Energy

Copyright © 1988, Raintree Publishers Inc.

Translated by Alison Taurel

Library of Congress Number: 87-28699

1 2 3 4 5 6 7 8 9 0   91 90 89 88

Printed and bound in the United States of America.

Library of Congress Cataloging in Publication Data

Energy.

   (Science and its secrets)
   Includes index.
   Summary: Explores the various types, uses, and
development of energy throughout the world.
   1. Power resources—Juvenile literature   [1. Power
resources]   I. Series.
TJ163.23.E5   1988   621.042—dc19   87-28699
ISBN 0-8172-3076-9 (lib. bdg.)
ISBN 0-8172-3093-9 (softcover)

ENERGY

Raintree Publishers — Milwaukee

Contents

INTRODUCTION

What does the word *energy* mean?

The cartoon character Popeye gets quick energy and super-strength from eating spinach. Actually, food cannot give instant strength. But people do get energy from food.

The word *energy* is often used in today's world. For example, people say that a person who makes quick decisions or is always on the go is "full of energy." Sometimes you get up in the morning feeling good. You are ready to play a game of football, basketball, or tennis. Then you are "full of energy," too. By the end of the game, you have run, jumped, and passed the ball. You go home tired, just wanting to eat and sleep. In a word, you are out of energy.

The idea of energy is probably familiar to you. When doing your chores, playing ball, or driving in a nail, you are doing work. To do these things, you are using energy. Simply put, energy is the ability to do work. Here, work means moving something against a resisting force. Any system or body that can produce work has energy.

Coal, when burning, can make a steam machine work. The wind can be used to mill grain. Water currents can also produce work. Coal, petroleum, and gas all supply energy. Even wind, tides, currents, waterfalls, and the heat of the sun's rays are sources of energy.

People have learned to use these sources of energy. With them, people complete all sorts of tasks.

From where does the human body get energy?

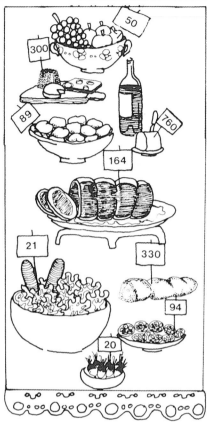

Food supplies the human body with energy.

You probably know the cartoon hero Popeye. Whenever Popeye needs superhuman strength, he quickly downs a can of spinach. In reality, no foods can give you such instant energy and strength. But the human body does get its energy from food. Food gives the body energy it needs to function.

Food is made up of nourishing substances called nutrients. These can be divided into three main groups: sugars, fats, and proteins. By eating, you take these nutrients into your body. But they are in a raw, or unusable, form. They must be broken down, or digested. Your body does this. It changes the food into simple sugar, fat, and protein products. These are then stored in millions of cells that make up the body. These cells are carried through the bloodstream. They are taken to different parts of the body where energy is needed. Some of the energy will be used to heat the body or build its tissues. Some will be used in making the muscles work.

People's bodies are always using energy. You are probably sitting quietly now as you read this book. Do you think you are not active? You are actually using energy without even knowing it. You are breathing. Your heart is beating, moving blood through your body. Every cell of your body is making chemical changes (as they do all day long). All of these things use energy.

A person's food intake must meet his or her needs. A mason or a lumberjack uses a great amount of energy. The food they eat must be richer than that of many people. People with less physical jobs use less energy. They may not need as much food as the lumberjack or mason. A dietician is a person who knows how to adapt people's diets to their needs.

People long dreamed of having a motor-powered vehicle such as this one. This 1690 sketch shows one inventor's idea of a steam-driven vehicle. Learning to convert energy made many of these dreams possible.

How is energy converted?

Imagine someone gives you a can of gasoline. What can you use it for if you don't have a car? Scientists face such problems all the time. Many energy sources are not directly usable. Examples of this are a layer of oil or a coal mine. Both are sources of energy. Neither can be used "as is." Like food coming into people's bodies, these sources must be changed to be used. When the source is changed, or converted, the energy is given off.

To change them, an energy converter must be used. This is a device that changes energy from one form into another. Energy converters are quite varied. Some are very simple. The pedal of your bike is one. It carries your power to the bicycle wheels. The blade of a waterwheel is another example. This converter uses the energy of falling water to turn the huge wheel. The turning wheel then does the work. Waterwheels can run all sorts of machinery. For example, a wheel may run a mill, which grinds grain into flour. But some converters are much more complex. Steam, gasoline, and electrical engines are examples of complex converters. These can make machines work or make vehicles move.

Even the human body has converters. These converters, which make people's muscles and brain cells work, are more puzzling. Scientists are far from understanding exactly how they work.

In industry, converters work with energy from natural sources. These energy forms are changed into mechanical or electrical energy. Electrical energy brings the world heat, light, and power. Mechanical energy moves machines and other things. But industry's converters have one major flaw. They change only forty percent of a source's energy. The rest is lost in heat that disappears into the atmosphere.

However, these converters have been improved in the last twenty years. Many of them can now change energy from different sources directly into electrical energy. And this can be done with no heat loss at all. An example of this new kind of converter is the solar battery.

How is energy measured?

Energy is often measured in units known as foot-pounds. One foot-pound is the amount of work done in moving an object one foot against a one pound force. If you lift a five pound weight four feet off the ground, you are using twenty foot-pounds of energy. In the metric system, energy is measured in joules.

Horsepower is another measurement concerning energy. But it is a measure of power, not of energy itself. Power is not the same as energy. Energy, you will remember, is the ability to do work. Power is how quickly you do it. Mechanical power is measured in units called horsepower. The term was first suggested by James Watt, a Scottish engineer. Watt suggested the term when working with the newly invented steam engine. Doubtful farmers probably asked how many horses a steam engine could replace. To make a comparison, Watt measured the amount of work a horse did in eight hours.

Many types of power are now measured in units called watts.

Certain energy-producing materials must be moved long distances. A system of pipes is often the best way to move these. These pipelines run across deserts, over mountains, and under rivers and lakes. They often carry substances such as water, natural gas, and petroleum.

What are the secrets of energy?

In some countries, people still use the energy of animals.

There are many different kinds of energy. These include solar energy, chemical energy, electrical energy, mechanical energy, nuclear energy, and others. As you have seen already, energy is very important to human life. Because of its importance to people, it can be very interesting to study. But there are two secrets to energy. Knowing these secrets will make studying it easier.

The first secret is that any form of energy can be changed into any other form. No matter what form energy takes, all are equal. You have proof of this every day. Take a flashlight into a dark room. Flick the switch, and the flashlight shoots light into the darkness. The battery's chemical energy has instantly been changed into light energy. Another example is a musician. Energy in the musician's fingers powers an instrument. This energy is changed into sound energy when the instrument plays. Even television sounds and images come from an energy change. From electrical energy, the television is full of light and sound.

Does this still seem amazing? Rub your hands together, wind some wire, and saw a piece of wood. Your hands, the wire, and the wood will all grow warm. In each case, mechanical energy has been changed into thermal energy.

The second secret is that energy never disappears. Although it can change forms, it is never created and never destroyed. It is simply converted from one form to another. All sorts of changes are possible. For example, bring a kettle of water to a boil. Then turn off the heat beneath it. The water will slowly cool. It may seem that the heat energy is lost or has disappeared. Actually, it has just spread out in the air.

All of modern science is based on this fact. No energy can be made without using an equal amount of another energy form. In other words, in producing one form of energy, another is consumed.

The steam engine also made the locomotive possible. Richard Trevithick invented the steam locomotive in England in 1804. The first locomotive was built in the United States twenty-one years later.

SOLAR ENERGY

How does the sun's heat reach earth?

The sun is a huge, glowing ball of gases. Its diameter is about 109 times that of the earth. The sun is a constantly changing mass. Sometimes, glowing fountains of gas can be seen shooting into the sky. These fountains, called flares, are a result of the sun's activity.

The sun's surface temperature is about 10,000°F (5,500°C). Its center is much hotter. There, temperatures reach 27,000,000°F (15,000,000°C). Energy is being made there every second. This is what makes the sun glow. About three-fourths of the sun's mass is hydrogen gas. This gas is under much pressure from the upper layers. Together, the heat and pressure change the hydrogen into another gas. This gas is called helium. The change sends out a great amount of energy. This energy is in the forms of heat and light.

The sun is the earth's most important source of energy. Without its heat and light, life could not exist. It would always be dark. The temperature would vary from too hot to too cold. Life could not exist.

But the sun does send heat and light. Its rays reach the earth in about eight minutes and twenty seconds. The earth's atmosphere traps the heat. Most of its light passes through the atmosphere, falling on the earth's surface. The light also warms the earth. But the heat it creates does not easily escape through the atmosphere. In this way, the earth is warmed by the sun. This is called the greenhouse effect, because the glass roof of a greenhouse traps heat in the same way. The glass lets sunlight in to heat the plants, but it does not allow the heat to escape.

The sun also gives off other rays besides visible light and heat. These include radio waves, ultraviolet rays, and X-rays. Both ultraviolet rays and X-rays can be harmful. The invisible ultraviolet rays are particularly strong. They can burn the skin. Luckily nature has given people a pigment to protect their skin. It is very important to people living in tropical regions. The earth's atmosphere also helps protect people from these invisible rays.

A solar flare, in the shape of a wheel, is seen from the Sacramento Observatory (United States).

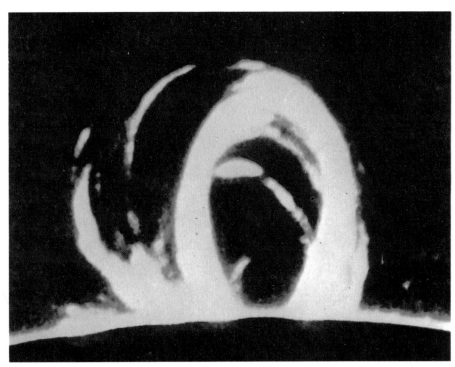

Can people live long without the sun?

The sun is the earth's main source of light and heat. It is also the source of all life. The sun makes it possible for plants to grow. Because of the sun, the earth produces millions of tons of grain and fruit every year. It is also the sun which controls the reproduction of most animals. Most animals mate according to the cycle of the seasons.

The sun is also important to people. For one thing, people eat both plants and animals. For another, the sun increases good health. It causes people's bodies to make vitamins. One of these vitamins, vitamin D, makes strong bones. The sun's rays are even used in medicine. Treatment known as heliotherapy fights against rickets. Rickets is a sickness in the development of the bones.

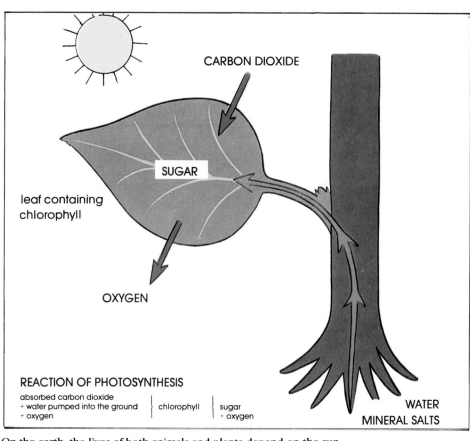

REACTION OF PHOTOSYNTHESIS

absorbed carbon dioxide + water pumped into the ground + oxygen	chlorophyll	sugar + oxygen

On the earth, the lives of both animals and plants depend on the sun.

The sun was always a symbol of worship.

The sun is also the source of oxygen in the earth's atmosphere. It was created over the course of millions of years. Oxygen is a result of a very important chemical reaction. This reaction, known as photosynthesis, occurs in green plants. Energy from light, water, and carbon dioxide are all absorbed by the plant. These things are changed into food for the plant. Oxygen is given off in the process.

Thus, plants replace the oxygen people use in breathing. Their work saves people and animals from suffocating. That is why it is important to preserve the forests. Keeping green areas in cities will help, too. If each person planted a tree each year, the air would be better.

Finally, almost all energy sources on earth begin with the sun's rays. Plants use sunlight to make food. Animals get energy from eating the plants. People eat both plants and animals. Energy sources such as oil, coal, and natural gas also come from the sun. These "stored up" energy sources are formed by decaying plant and animal matter. This process takes millions of years. With some energy sources, the sun is directly involved. Its heat moves the wind and the water. These are also sources of energy.

Solar homes gather energy from the sun. Devices known as solar collectors do the gathering. Solar heat can be used to cook food and heat homes. It can even generate electricity.

What is it like to live in a solar home?

In the 1920s, solar water heaters were used in several thousand homes throughout the country. They were used mainly in Florida and the Southwest. Solar power was popular only for a time, though. As electricity became available, people lost interest in it.

Today, solar power is being taken more seriously. In warmer countries such as Japan and Israel, many solar heaters are at work. In Japan, 2.5 million homes use solar heaters. Israel has about 200,000.

This method of heating is actually quite simple. Gardeners and florists have used it for years in their greenhouses. As you know, the idea behind solar heat is even called the "greenhouse effect."

Solar homes are built in a special way. They use a device called a solar collector to gather the sun's energy. A collector is a large glassed area. It is usually a shallow box with a lid of glass. This lid is called the glazing. It allows the sun's rays to pass through it into the collector. It also prevents heat from escaping. Inside, the sunlight hits an absorber. This is a dark, plate-like surface. The absorber's job is to take in, or absorb, the sun's heat. The heat is then taken into the storage area. A storage area can be made of stone or brick. It can also be a tank filled with water.

To heat the house, the stored heat must be spread around the house. Some solar energy systems rely on the heated air's natural movements. This type is known as passive solar energy. Another system uses pumps and fans to spread the heat. This is called active solar energy. Both methods are used in solar homes.

Is solar energy something new?

Many people think that solar energy is a new idea. It is not. The term solar energy simply refers to the light and heat from the sun. People have been using solar energy since ancient times.

The Greeks may have been among the first to use solar energy. Historians tell of the Greek mathematician, Archimedes, who used the sun's energy in battle. According to the story, a Roman fleet made a surprise attack on the Greeks. Archimedes knew the Greeks were outnumbered. As the ships came closer, their black sails gave him an idea. He had his soldiers aim their bright shields at the Roman ships. The shields reflected the sunlight like mirrors. The sun's rays were so strong that the Roman ships caught fire.

They burned before they reached land.

Experts do not know if this story is true. But it is certainly true that solar energy can be harnessed. That is, it can be captured and used. Both the Greeks and the Romans used the sun's heat. Often, their homes, buildings, and public gathering places were built facing south. The sun's rays are strongest from this direction. Their well planned building sites took advantage of this.

The American Indians also considered the sun when building homes. They built their homes of thick clay. The clay is useful for absorbing and holding heat. More recently, people learned to use the sun to power machinery. Some things such as solar pumps and

furnaces existed in the 1700s. By the 1800s, inventors were working with solar steam engines.

Today, scientists continue to work with solar energy. They hope to find better ways of gathering and storing the sun's energy. The steam engine made steam power cheap and plentiful. One day soon, science may do the same for solar energy.

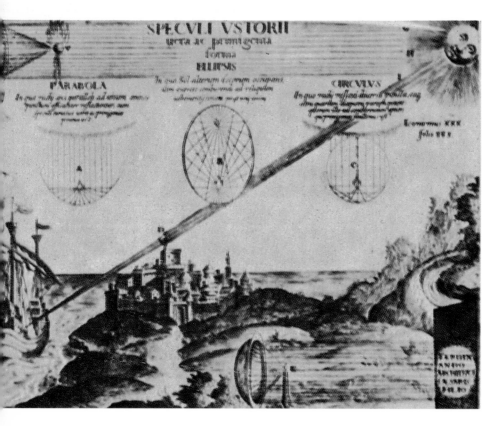

According to legend, the Greek mathematician Archimedes harnessed the sun's heat to set fire to enemy ships. True or not, the story captured the imaginations of many scientists throughout the years. The idea of controlling this powerful energy source was fascinating. Many scientists put much time into this idea, developing plans and conducting experiments.

How does a solar furnace work?

Solar energy can be used to create very high temperatures. This is done with a device that concentrates the sun's rays. The solar furnace is a device for doing just this. It was used already in ancient times. The solar furnace works much like Archimedes' mirrors. It concentrates the sun's rays at one point. Today, solar furnaces are used on a much larger scale. They serve scientists working in high-temperature research.

The first European solar furnace was built in the 1960s. French scientists built it in the Pyrenees Mountains. There, the air is clean and clear, even in the winter. This furnace reaches temperatures of 5,975°F (3,300°C). Similar furnaces have been built in the United States, Japan, and Russia.

The huge furnace of Odeillo-Font-Romeu in France was built in 1970. This furnace has many parts. It begins with sixty-three mobile mirrors, called heliostats. These heliostats are laid out in tiers, or terraces, on the European hillside. Each has a surface of 484 square feet (45 square meters). Together, the mirrors follow the sun's path. They reflect its rays toward a huge curved mirror. This mirror is called a parabolic mirror. It is made of nine thousand sheets of plate glass. The mirror concentrates the energy in a small area in front of it. This, to be exact, is the furnace. Simple furnaces such as this can create heats as high as 4,900°F (2,700°C).

The simple greenhouse effect creates temperatures between 212° and 302°F (100° to 150°C). To reach higher temperatures, the sun's rays must be concentrated. That means they must be directed toward one point, or focus. Archimedes and the Greek soldiers did this with their shields. A modern device known as the solar furnace also does this.

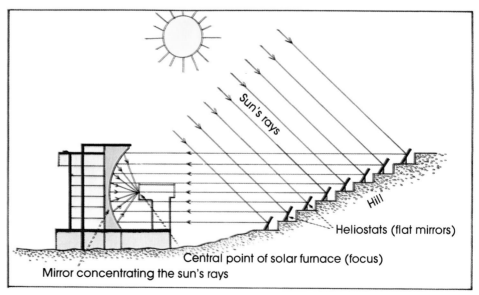

Sun's rays

Hill

Heliostats (flat mirrors)

Central point of solar furnace (focus)

Mirror concentrating the sun's rays

Can solar energy meet the world's needs?

This picture shows Skylab I as photographed from Skylab II. The space station's large panels were actually solar battery panels. These panels provided electricity for the station.

The solar energy available in one year is enormous. It is about ten thousand times greater than the world's present needs. It is even more than what the globe will need by the twenty-first century. But scientists do not yet know how to harness this energy. Storing, moving, and converting solar energy is still a problem.

Solar converters called solar cells were invented in 1964. These change solar energy directly into electricity. This change can be done in large power stations. But for this, very large solar receptors must be built. Receptors gather the sun's rays. These receptors would measure 1 to 3 sq. miles (3 to 8 sq. kilometers). Of course, these are too big to build in cities. Instead, they must be built in sites that offer constant sunlight.

Solar converters are still only a modest source of energy. Their cost is still high. An equal amount of electrical energy costs much less to produce. But scientists expect solar energy to become more practical in the future. One possible project calls for putting a huge satellite in orbit. This satellite would be shaped like a butterfly. Each of its wings would be a mass of solar cells. The satellite would be six miles long by three miles wide. It would weigh ten thousand tons.

But already there are many uses for these solar converters. In Africa, for example, solar pumps are being used. These pumps are designed to bring underground water to the surface. This has changed the ways of life for certain villages. This is especially true in areas that do not get much rain. There, the pumps can be used to supply drinking water for people and animals. They also supply water for croplands.

Solar converters are also being used in Israel. This country has little fresh water. There, solar energy is used to purify sea water. Similar experiments are being done in Turkey, Chile, and Algeria.

So why isn't solar energy being used to run cars? It has been tried. Experiments were done as early as 1912. But it took ten hours to gather enough energy to drive the car one hour. Then it could only go 25 miles per hour (40 km). The results would not be much better today. But there will come a day when they are.

People began to experiment with solar cars as early as 1912. A solar collector on the roof captured the sun's rays.

COAL

How long has coal been in use?

It is hard to say when coal was first used in Europe. But in 1,000 B.C., the Chinese were already using it. They used it to bake porcelain. Coal is also mentioned in ancient Greek history.

In the western countries, forests were already drained of their wood by the twelfth century. Lumber was in great demand for building. Ships and houses had to be built. The houses had to be heated. The cost of wood went up as the demand did. No doubt people were already looking for another means of heat.

One legend from Belgium tells how coal came into use. According to the story, an old man happened by a poor blacksmith's shop. Because wood was scarce, the blacksmith had no fire for his forge. The old man told the blacksmith to go to a nearby mountain. "There," the old man said, "you will find veins of a kind of black earth." This earth, he said, would make the forge work. The blacksmith followed the advice. Finding coal, he became a rich man.

But the use of coal did not spread easily. Many Europeans saw coal as a dirty fuel. They objected to it because it dirtied clothes and made women unattractive. It was also said to poison the air and waste the lungs. In France, scientists protested its use. In England, the king himself forbade it. Worse yet, the mines smelled of sulfur. Many people believed this meant

An 1860 engraving shows coal miners being lowered into a mine.

that the devil had passed through there. Using coal for heating, then, was a test of courage. It went against public opinion, and in some cases, the law.

Slowly, the forests began to grow again. But by that time, many people had come to their senses about using coal. By the seventeenth century, coal had replaced wood in many ways. It was used for heating in many places. It was also used in breweries, glass-making, brick-making, and many other businesses.

In five hundred years, coal mining had grown greatly. At first, people mined coal from shallow surface holes. Before long, the

real mine shafts were used. These shafts, supported by beams, were very dangerous. The dangers of explosions, cave-ins, or fires were great. There was also the danger of drowning when water rushed into the shaft. Pumps were put to work non-stop.

By the beginning of the eighteenth century, coal was put to use in the tall furnaces. This marked the beginning of the Industrial Revolution. England was rich in coal deposits. As coal's use grew, so did the country's wealth. With the invention of the steam engine, even more coal was needed. This new energy source forever changed the world.

In the 1900s, horses were used in mine work.

How is coal formed?

Three hundred million years ago, the earth was covered by huge forests.

As the land sank, many plants died and began to decay. They formed layer after layer of decaying matter.

The forests caused the land to sink greatly in certain areas.

Eventually, these layers of decayed plant matter were turned into coal.

The outlines of ancient plants are often found in layers of sediment. These outlines, called fossils, were formed millions of years ago.

Millions of years ago, gigantic forests still covered the earth. In certain areas, these forests were covered over by water. The plants died and formed a thick layer of matter. As this matter hardened, it became peat. Through time, the peat was covered by different layers of soil and sediment. Buried under heavy layers of sediment, the peat was protected from the air. Slowly, all of this plant matter began to change. From this change came coal.

Over millions of years, this process happened many times. Scientists know this from studying the different layers of a coal bed. Coal beds are also called coal seams or coal veins. But all simply refer to a deposit of coal. Many of these beds consist of two or more seams of coal. These seams are separated by layers of sediment. Each seam shows where one coal-producing mass of plants formed over a buried one.

Coal seams generally lie parallel to the earth's surface. Coal found near the surface, then, is generally newer coal. But this is not always true. Some beds have been disturbed by movements in the earth. These may be tilted so that they lie almost vertical to the surface. Other seams are broken by faults in the earth. These sections can take on very different forms. In many of these cases, the order of the layers is confused. A very old coal seam may end up near the surface. A very young layer may end up buried.

Coal mining is not always done in underground tunnels. Strip mining, also called open cast mining, is done at the surface. There miners dig the coal from an exposed seam. Here a peat bog is mined for coal.

How do peat, lignite, bituminous coal, and anthracite differ?

As decaying matter becomes coal, it passes through several stages. These stages are peat, lignite, bituminous coal, and anthracite. During this process, the substance's makeup changes. But one thing remains stable—the element carbon.

All forms of coal contain carbon. This element, in combination with others, is what makes coal burn. In fact, the amount of carbon coal has determines its stage.

Peat, as you already know, forms when layers of plant matter harden. When taken from the bottom of dried swamps, peat has very little carbon in it. It has so little carbon that it smokes when burned. Peat leaves behind great amounts of ash.

Huge deposits of peat, called peat bogs, are found in Ireland. In one very poor area, peasants help themselves to the peat. They cut it in pieces and load it into baskets. Donkeys carry these baskets to the peasants' homes. The peat will heat their homes through the winter. Peat is also used as a fuel in factories. For this, it is cut into huge bricks. From the bogs, the peat is taken by donkey cart to the main roads. There it is picked up and transported to the factories.

Lignite comes from peat deposits that have been under much pressure. The pressure comes from new layers of sediment and plant matter. Lignite is easily recognized. It is not as black or as dense as later coals. It is also more loose-grained and has less car-bon. Because of this, it does not heat as well as later coal forms. Lignite often comes from Russian and German mines.

Still greater pressure changes lignite into coal. At this point, coal is called bituminous coal. Bituminous coal is the most common type of coal. It is very black and sooty. This coal has much carbon and burns well.

The oldest stage of coal is known as anthracite. Anthracite is the hardest of coals. It is very shiny and does not dirty your hands when you touch it. Anthracite is also rich in carbon. Because of this, it burns slowly and leaves no ash behind. It gives off great heat and lasts a long time.

What is an underground coal mine like?

Imagine touring a coal mine. From far away, you first see huge black hills. These hills, called slag heaps, are leftover materials from the mining operations. Next you arrive at the bank of the mine. The bank is the large ground area above the mines. Any buildings or mining materials can be found there. In among the buildings is an iron tower. This tower raises and lowers the elevators, or cages, into the shaft. Today, powerful electric machines run the lifts.

Lifts are used to take both people and machines to the coal. They also take coal to the surface. Because the coal is found between layers of sediment, the shafts are often deep. Deeper mines have air shafts as well.

It takes about a year to dig a mine about 1,640 feet (500 m) deep. The shafts are usually dug in pairs. These shafts run from the surface to the coal bed. One shaft will serve the miners and their equipment. The other will be used to haul coal out. The shafts are joined at different depths by horizontal tunnels. These tunnels, called galleries, are sometimes made using small explosives.

Examine the picture on this page. This mine has two main shafts and galleries. In some places, the galleries cut through the coal seam. There, the earth and rocks are removed, and two shorter galleries, or tunnels, are formed. The lower of these is called the "lower track." The other is the "upper track." This is a fairly common example of a mine.

Imagine what it was like to be a miner years ago. In the early days, conditions were very bad. Men, women, and children worked up to eighteen hours in cramped tunnels. They did all their work with a pick axe. Often they had to move forward on their stomachs or backs. The air was poor and cave-ins were not uncommon. Even the lighting in early mines was dangerous. At the time, the mines were lit with candles. This often led to explosions when gas was present. In the 1800s, unions formed to change these conditions. The United Mine Workers of America was formed in 1890. These unions worked toward better conditions and setting up safety standards. Because of them, mine conditions did improve.

This cutaway view of an underground coal mine shows many connecting shafts and tunnels.

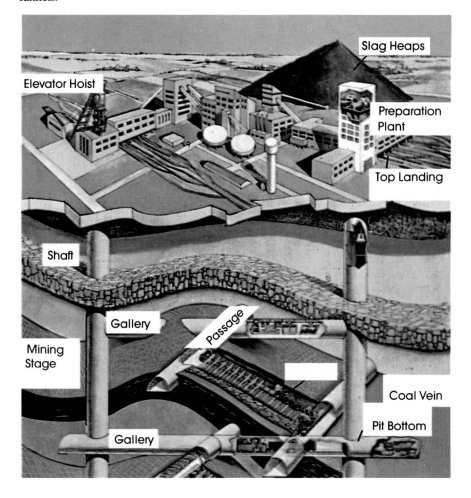

Elevator Hoist

Slag Heaps

Preparation Plant

Top Landing

Shaft

Gallery

Passage

Mining Stage

Coal Vein

Pit Bottom

Gallery

How is coal processed?

Some coal is used just as it comes from the mine. Nothing is done to this coal before it is shipped to the buyer. In the industry, this coal is called run-of-mine coal. But some buyers want a certain type of coal for their uses. They have requirements, or standards, which the coal must meet. This coal must be processed, or cleaned, before the buyers will accept it. Cleaning removes impurities such as ash and sulfur from the coal.

There are three steps to cleaning coal: sorting, washing, and drying. In sorting, a screening device separates the coal by size. The machine separates them into three sizes: coarse, medium, and fine coal chunks. Extremely large chunks of coal are broken up in a huge crusher. The ground pieces are then resorted.

Next comes the washing step. Still separated by size, the coal is moved into a washing tank. At this point, water is mixed with the coal. This is done to separate the impurities from the coal. The process will remove most of the remaining ash. The sulfur, however, is closely linked with the carbon. Only small amounts of that will be removed. Finally, the coal must be dried. After the washing, the coal has taken on a lot of water. This must be removed. Otherwise, the coal will not burn as well.

A machine known as a cutting machine is often used in coal mining. The machine's rotating drum has many spikes.

How are coal pellets made?

During cutting, cleaning, and transporting, some of the coal has been reduced to fine particles. These are called smalls. As dust, the coal is of little value. It cannot be used in this form. So this dust is mixed with a binding substance. The dust and the binder soon become a paste.

This paste is then heated. When it is very hot, it is rolled between two wheels. The wheels are lined with many oval or round holes, like an egg carton. The paste is squashed between these wheels, or presses. The paste is formed into small, hard balls. These coal pellets can then be used in stoves, smokestacks, and boilers.

Smelting furnaces are huge ovens used in making metals. Some are as tall as ten-story buildings.

How is coke used in smelting furnaces?

A red-hot batch of coke is released from a coking oven. It will then be taken to another part of the plant to cool. Coke is made by heating coal in an airtight oven.

As its name suggests, the smelting furnace is a huge oven. It is used to process metals. Processing metals is a lot like cleaning coal. Both processes are meant to separate the valuable substance from any impurities in it. In smelting, metals are taken from their original ores. The original ores also contain a lot of sand and rocks. Smelting creates pure metals, such as iron and steel. These metals are then used in many different industries. They are used to make rail tracks, frames for bridges, girders for buildings, sheet metal, etc.

Coke is a hard, grayish material. It is light and porous. That is, it is full of many small holes, like a pumice stone. These holes develop as the coke is formed. It is made by heating soft natural coals. These coals, called "fat coals," are heated in tall, narrow cooking ovens. These ovens are also air-tight. Without air, the coal will not burn. The heat simply changes its form.

Coke is an important part of the smelting process. Take the smelting of iron ore, for example. This rock is very rich in iron. But there are also many other materials, or impurities, in the ore. To get at the valuable iron, the ore must be smelted. To do this, iron ore, coke, and limestone are fed into a furnace. As the coke burns, it releases gases and heat. Both are useful in the process. The gas, first of all, purifies the metal. It separates the iron from the other materials in the ore. After that, heat from the coke melts everything. The impurities are lighter than the iron. They will float on top of the iron. This makes it easy to remove them, leaving only the pure iron. Large amounts of coke are used this way every year.

How long will the earth's coal supply last?

The world has huge coal reserves. But they are spread unevenly from one country to the next. Russia and other socialist countries have the greatest amount of coal. Their reserves equal about sixty percent of the world's total reserves. The United States has about twenty percent of the world's reserves. Canada has eight percent. Europe has the smallest amount with less than two percent of the world's total.

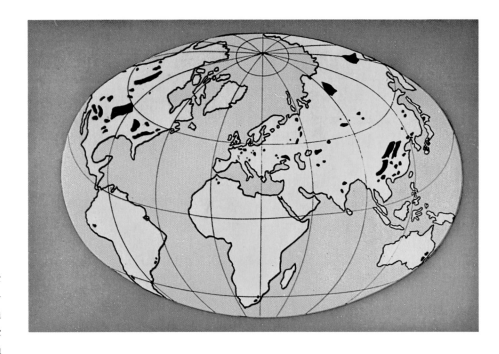

Coal was once the main source of energy. This fuel provided power for industrial nations through the nineteenth century. Since the early 1900s, however, petroleum and natural gas have been used heavily. Both of these substances are easy, available sources of heat and fuel. But they are also being used up quickly. For this reason, coal also continues to be a leading fuel. It is plentiful and has great heating value. But it, too, is a limited resource. In other words, it will not last forever.

In some countries, smelting needs and thermal power stations use great amounts of coal. For these two uses alone, a country may use two-thirds of all its available coal. The rest of the coal is used in small industry.

The world has large coal deposits. They are spread unevenly over the world. They can be found on every continent. Some are even found off the coasts in the ocean. These deposits, however, are not yet very useful. Scientists have not yet come up with a good way to mine these deposits. Other deposits are found far below the earth's surface. These are also difficult to mine. They are also very expensive. Sometimes, it is actually cheaper for a country to import coal than to mine its own.

Since 1973, world coal production has increased. Most of the deposits in the United States, Russia, and China are mined in surface mines. This method is more successful, but it is hard on the land. Surface mines put out three to ten times more coal than underground mines. The working conditions are also better.

Despite increased mining, reserves are great. They are thought to be four or five times greater than the supply of petroleum. One day, coal may take the place of petroleum. During the second World War, petroleum was short.

The Germans learned to make gasoline from coal to meet their needs. Today, car engines in South Africa are fed with a coal gasoline. This gasoline must be an improvement of the Germans' fuel of forty years ago.

But as coal's uses increase, the reserves will begin to run dry. At present, coal is used for only a quarter of the world's energy needs. This may be enough to meet the world's needs for another two hundred years. It may even last as long as a thousand years. It depends on many things.

PETROLEUM

What is a petroleum reserve?

The word *petroleum* comes from two Latin words that mean "rock oil." People gave it this name when they found it seeping up through cracks in the rocks. Today, petroleum is often called oil.

To understand how oil is formed, imagine the planet five or six million years ago. Then, the ocean covered many parts of the earth. Tiny creatures, called plankton, lived in the shallow water and along the coasts. When these creatures died, they settled to the ocean bottom. Their remains built a thick layer. Mud and other sediment settled on top of this matter. The sediments protected the plankton remains from air. Their great weight pressed the plankton into tight layers. During this process, the plant and animal remains became oil.

Was this change the result of strong pressure and high temperatures? Was it due to bacteria in the airless environment? No one knows for sure how petroleum formed. But many experts accept the plankton-decay idea as a possible solution. This idea is known as the organic theory.

As the oil formed, it seeped from the mud beds into the layers of rock. There it was absorbed by porous rocks. Porous rocks are rocks with small holes, or pores, in them. Over years, layers of other rocks formed around the porous rock. Some layers were made of impermeable, or solid, rock. Nothing, including the oil, could pass through these layers. Changes in the earth's crust shifted the rock layers. This left the oil sealed in underground pockets, called traps. These traps formed the reserves from which oil is now taken.

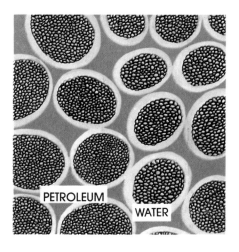

PETROLEUM   WATER

Petroleum is never found in one vast pool, like an underground lake. It is found in various underground structures, known as traps. Traps form when petroleum seeps into porous rocks. These rocks are surrounded by layers of other materials. As the earth's crust changes, these layers seal the petroleum in traps.

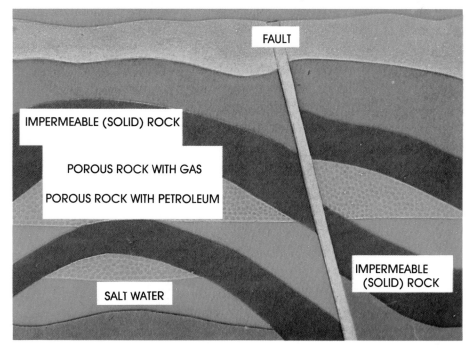

FAULT

IMPERMEABLE (SOLID) ROCK

POROUS ROCK WITH GAS

POROUS ROCK WITH PETROLEUM

SALT WATER

IMPERMEABLE (SOLID) ROCK

Who drilled the first oil well?

People have used petroleum since ancient times. Years ago, they collected it in small containers from where it oozed from the ground. In America, the Indians, pharmacists, and doctors used their share of it as medicine. For hundreds of years the Indians had used petroleum to treat skin sicknesses, breathing difficulties, etc. It was not long before someone realized its other uses. Before long, petroleum had replaced whale oil for lighting. The oil lamp was born.

Most experts credit Edwin L. Drake with starting the oil industry on a big scale. In 1858, the "Colonel," as he was known, was hired by the Seneca Oil Company. This group of businessmen became interested in oil as a fuel. Unfortunately, no one had yet invented a good way to get it out of the ground. They hired Drake to drill a well near Titusville, Pennsylvania.

Together with Billy Smith, a well-digger, Drake dug one pit after another. The men used a wooden rig and a steam-run drill. But each pit they dug was threat-

An 1859 photograph shows the first successful oil well drilled in the United States. It was drilled by Edwin L. "Colonel" Drake in Titusville, Pennsylvania. It was this well that launched the oil industry.

ened by water and cave-ins. Finally Drake ran an iron pipe deep into the ground and drilled inside it. The pipe acted as a casing. It kept Drake's path clear for drilling. About a year later, Drake and "Uncle Billy" had dug a well 69.5 feet (21.2 m) deep. On August 27, 1859, the oil suddenly swept up the shaft. The discouraged Drake had nearly abandoned the well.

What was the black gold rush?

Businessmen quickly realized the wealth that the thick black liquid could bring. Drilling for oil was much like panning for gold. Some people made fortunes in a few minutes. Others were ruined just as quickly. For this reason, oil became known as "black gold." The rush to the oil wells was often called the "black gold rush."

Oil-hungry people left their homes to join the rush. They abandoned their families, forgot their jobs, and dropped everything to join the adventure. Very few of them were successful. Many others, after abandoning all they had, eventually gave up or died trying.

Drilling for oil was risky business. An oil man's luck often changed over night. A well that was flowing one day might quit the next. Often a rival had dug too close, capturing a neighbor's "rock oil."

One tale is of an oilman named Old Shaw. In 1862, Old Shaw was among those ruined while searching for oil. Though his clothes and boots had worn thin, Shaw persisted. One day, he went to a shop in town. There he asked for a pair of boots on credit. The owner refused. Old Shaw returned to his drill, swearing to abandon it.

At his well, he once again took up his tools. Attacking the rock, he heard a whistling, bubbling sound. In a moment, the well was gushing. The news spread fast.

Shaw was standing before the well, his boots gaping, when the store owner showed up.

"My dear Mr. Shaw," the shopkeeper said, "isn't there anything in my place that you need? I beg you, don't hesitate to tell me."

You can imagine Shaw's response. Overnight he had gone from a beggar to "Mr. Shaw." Now the old pioneer could get boots at whatever price he wanted, wherever he wanted. Unfortunately, Old Shaw died two months later. He was overcome by gases as he went down into his well. Shaw's tale may or may not be true. Its importance is the "rags to riches" story it tells. Unfortunately, the "black gold rush" took more people from riches to rags.

An 1860 photograph shows Titusville as one mass of derricks. When Drake's well first gushed, the company sold the oil for twenty dollars a barrel. Because of the "black gold rush," oil soon dropped to ten cents a barrel.

Seismic prospecting is done in Abu Dhabi. This method uses weak dynamite charges. They are set off just below the surface. The shock waves are recorded and studied. From the recordings, experts can locate oil deposits.

What is an oil prospector?

An oil prospector's job is to determine the location of future wells. This is difficult. Scientists have no way of knowing exactly where petroleum has formed. But they do know what kinds of rock formations are likely to contain oil.

Once a prospector chooses a likely spot, tests and studies are done. The rock layers are studied for origin and type. Surface maps are made. Samples of the underground layers are taken with a drill. These are called core samples.

If the area still seems positive, the prospector may use one of several methods. In the first, the prospector sets off small underground dynamite charges. Shock waves from the explosion are reflected in different ways. These will show how deep the rock layers lie. They will also help the prospector determine the types of rock layers.

Another method calls for studying the magnetic or gravitational pull of the land. Different rocks give different gravitational or magnetic readings. The differences from one area to another are often great. They will indicate when an area's conditions are good for oil formation.

The most elaborate method uses electrodes. These electrodes are planted in the earth. They measure the behavior of different layers when exposed to electrical currents.

Today, many of these tests can be done at once. The information from the tests is fed into a computer. The computer will then determine the deposit's location. This first phase of oil drilling requires much patience.

What happens "in the shadow of the derricks"?

Now the prospector has decided on an area to drill. Soon a crew of workers, called rig builders, will arrive. They will build a huge metal framework called a derrick. The derrick will stand directly over the spot where the well is to be drilled. Derricks generally stand between 80 and 200 feet (24 to 61 m) high. These support the drills.

The most common method of drilling is known as rotary drilling. A rotary drill works in much the same way as a carpenter's drill. Like a carpenter's drill, the rotary drill also has a drill bit. The drill bit spins around, or rotates, while pressing downward.

The drill bit is connected to a hollow shaft called the drill pipe. A drill pipe is a hollow steel tube about 30 feet (9 m) long. As it is turned, the drill bit also turns. The rotary drill moves about 3 feet (1 m) per minute in fairly soft ground. Soon the entire drill pipe has been dug into the ground. To continue, another shaft must be screwed to the top of the first. This procedure is repeated until the well is dug.

The drill pipe is very important to this method of drilling. Among other things, the pipe is also used

The cluster of control valves used to cap a well is often called a "Christmas tree."

to carry drilling mud. Drilling mud is a heavy liquid that is poured into the pipe. The drilling mud keeps the drill from overheating. It also keeps other liquids from getting into the well. Finally, it carries crushed rock and sediment to the surface.

Even so, a normal bit may dull or fall apart after several hundred feet of drilling. This distance may be even less if the earth is especially hard. For this reason, drillers use different bits for different types of rock. For hard rock layers, drillers use a rock bit. This bit has a group of rotating teeth on its end. A diamond may be used to cut through very hard rock.

Sometimes the pipes smash or the bit breaks. Then all the pieces must be removed from the well. Those that are not removed may slow the drill's progress. If they cannot be removed, the drill's course is changed.

The most modern drilling method also uses the drilling pipe. But in this method, only the drill bit turns. The pipe stays in one place. Drilling mud, forced into the tube, turns the drill bit at a great speed.

Whatever type of drilling is done, it is a long time before the first core sample is found. A core sample is a sample of the drilling mud that shows the presence of petroleum. It may be a year before this is found. When oil is found, the drill is pulled from the well. Only the casing remains. The weight of the drilling mud will control the flow until workers cap it. Later, a group of control valves is placed over the casing. This pyramid-shaped mass of tubes, levers, and pipes is often called a "Christmas tree." With it, the oil's flow can be controlled.

The derrick is the steel tower that holds the well-drilling equipment. Hanging from this derrick is a rock bit. The rock bit is known for its gear-like jagged teeth. These teeth are useful for cutting through very hard rock layers.

A pipeline is one way to move petroleum over a long distance.

Large ships, called tankers, are another method of moving petroleum. These tankers carry the oil across the oceans, along the coasts, and even on the Great Lakes.

How is crude oil transported?

Crude oil is a term for petroleum as it comes from the earth. For many uses, oil must be processed, or refined. This is done in a plant called a refinery. There the oil is turned into gasoline, diesel oil, and other useful products. Often, these refineries are far from where the crude oil is found. The oil must then be shipped to them. Pipelines and petroleum tankers are two means of doing this. With them, oil is moved from the field to refineries.

A pipeline is a system of pipes. Pipelines were first used in ancient times. The early Romans used a pipeline for distributing water through the city. The first oil pipeline in America was built in 1865. It carried oil from Titusville, Pennsylvania, to a railroad five miles away. It was not until after World War II that they appeared in Europe.

Pipelines are made of many steel pipes welded together. Often, each piece is 33 feet (10 m) long. When building on flat ground, the pipeline can be done quickly. The crew may complete as much as 3 miles (5 km) a day. But not all areas are so pleasant. Getting across a steep area, a river, or an arm of the sea slows this pace. Pipelines run across deserts, over mountains, and even under water.

A series of pumps powers the pipeline. The pumps, built at different distances along the line, may be from 31 to 186 miles (50 to 300 km) apart. These pumps force the oil to move through the pipes. At this moment, more than

124,000 miles (200,000 km) of pipeline criss-cross the world.

The first oil tanker dates back to 1886. It was a cargo vessel, able to carry only 5,500 tons of oil. Today's giant tankers can carry 550,000 tons. They are made up of several separate tanks. This lessens the risk at sea. Some of these tanks are self-powered. They can be steered toward different unloading areas.

This strange structure is found in the Arabian Gulf. It is an oil reservoir, or tank. This tank holds 105,000 cu. yards (80,000 cu m) of oil.

What is the "black tide"?

When the oil tanker empties its cargo, it rises in the water. The weight loss makes it less stable on the open sea. To right this, the ship's oil tanks are filled with water. This water mixes with a black substance left behind by the oil. This water is sometimes carelessly released into the oceans. This "black tide" eventually washes toward shore. Along the way, it kills many living things.

It is difficult to enforce proper emptying of these tankers. International agreements on the matter do exist. But many of them are simply ignored. Because of this, many of the oceans and seas have been dangerously polluted.

Even worse than this are accidentally caused black tides. These are brought about by storms, bad steering, explosions, boats running aground, etc. However they happen, the tanker then loses its cargo. This black tide is much more destructive.

The first major accident of this type happened in March, 1967. A tanker called the *Torrey-Canyon*

Oil spills on the oceans are also known as "black tides."

Black tides are responsible for the deaths of many marine animals. Birds struggle in the oil and die painful deaths on the beaches.

spilled 88,000 tons of oil into the English Channel. This black tide battered the French coast of Brittany. Many similar accidents have happened since.

In January, 1976, a giant oil tanker set out from Brest, in Brittany, on its maiden voyage. The tanker, known as the *Olympic Bravery*, was carrying 330,600 tons of oil. It ran aground on the isle of Ouessent thirteen hours later. It remained there, without help. On March 13, there was a huge storm. The great tanker was broken in two on the rocks. Tons of crude oil escaped its holds. The oil spread over the sea.

Helicopters followed the movements of this black mass. The speed of the currents rapidly moved it toward the coast. It was a disaster. Rocks were covered with the sticky oil. The beaches disappeared. Birds desperately circled in the sky. Many were covered with the oil and died.

Finally, the army was called in to help. Soldiers fought the tide for weeks. Exhausted, they cleaned up the mess, rock by rock, beach by beach. Many chemicals were used to break up the oily mess. This poisoned the marine life for several years.

It can be even worse than that. Oil tankers are built even bigger in different shipyards in the Atlantic. There is even talk of million-ton tankers in the future.

A diver inspects an offshore oil well.

What is offshore drilling?

—The year, 1965 . . . five platforms sink into the North Sea . . . doing millions of dollars worth of damage.

—April, 1976 . . . three scientists disappear while on a prospecting trip in the North Sea.

—April, 1977 . . . in the North Sea, oil escapes from Bravo platform and spreads over the sea.

On land, prospecting, drilling, and collecting oil is a challenge. At sea, this process, often called offshore drilling, can be nearly impossible. These random clips give you an idea of how difficult it can be. (See the picture of an offshore oil rig on page 24.)

The seismic method is often used to find oil deposits at sea. This method uses echoes caused by explosions to find the reserves. This is done with the use of hydrophones. A hydrophone is a device for listening to sound through water. Unfortunately, this system also picks up different sea sounds. This can cause inaccurate records. The oil sites can be difficult to find.

In offshore drilling, work goes on around the clock. The people work in eight-hour shifts with only the sea in sight. Often even this is masked by fog. On this job, there are no Saturdays or Sundays. Instead, workers are given a longer rest every few weeks.

In offshore wells, the ocean's depth is important. When it is about 164 feet (50 m) deep, the platform rests on "legs." Then, if the weather gets bad, the platform is raised. If the water is deeper, the platform is set on floats. It then looks like a water spider that runs on lakes and ponds in the summer.

About 660 to 980 feet (200 to 300 m) from the bottom is the drilling vessel. The most modern of these devices is "the Pelican." It was built in 1971 in France. The Pelican must stay in place even when the sea is rough.

Offshore drilling operations are carried on as though on land.

While drilling, the pipes must be screwed onto each other. The drill bits must be changed, etc. But drilling at sea adds extra problems. The oil must be kept from seeping into the ocean water. This can happen when the drill hits oil. It can also happen when the "Christmas tree" is being put in place.

Then there is the problem of transporting the oil. An underground pipeline can be used if the site is near the coast. Farther from the coast, manufactured islands can be used. These islands will support huge tanks of oil in open water. Oil tankers can load up from these tanks.

How do regular and super gasolines differ?

"Super or regular?"

You have probably heard this question when stopping at a gas station. The person pumping the gas has to know. Do you want super or regular gas in the gas tank? If you like starting off quickly or passing in a flash, ask for super gas. If you are more economical, ask for regular gas.

When taken from the ground, crude oil is a mixture of several things. In order, they are: bitumen fuels, gas-oil, paraffins, oils, kerosene, white-spirit, gasoline, and finally, the gases. No two crude oils are alike. Crude oil from the Middle East is rich in gasoline. That from the Sahara is rich in fuel.

Most gasoline is made by sep- arating the different products in petroleum. This is called refining. Ordinary gasoline is refined in a very few steps. Super gasoline is refined in several steps. Small amounts of various products are added to it. These products will improve an engine's quality.

One commonly added product is an antiknock fluid. Knocking happens when a gasoline mixture explodes suddenly as the spark plugs fire. This causes an engine's familiar "knocking" or "pinging." To run smoothly, some cars need a gasoline that resists knocking. A gasoline's ability to resist knocks is indicated by its octane number. This number shows how smoothly the gasoline will burn.

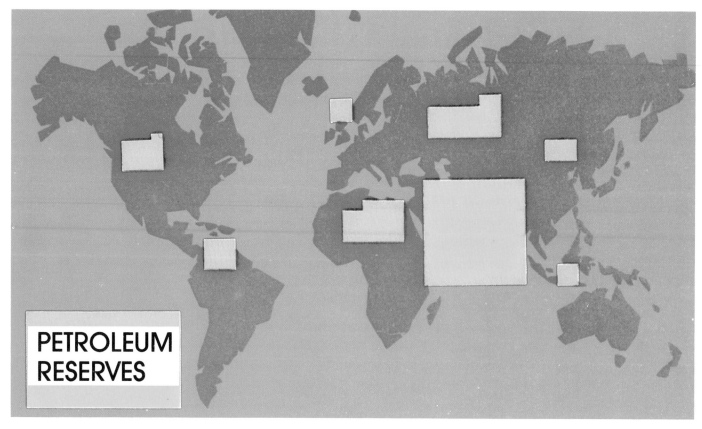

Most of the world's petroleum reserves are found in the areas highlighted on this map. They include: the Middle East-58%, Russia-13%, Africa-10%, Latin America-6.6%, the United States-6.6%, and Europe-1.8%.

Will there still be petroleum in the year 2000?

In this century, world use of petroleum has doubled every ten years. This explains why the earth is always being prospected. Close to 30,000 drillings take place each year. Since Colonel Drake's time, more than two million holes have been dug. These holes are just those in American soil.

Maybe you already know that petroleum will disappear from the planet first. This became clear back in 1973. Then, petroleum represented more than half of all fuel sources. Its use will stabilize in the next twenty years. Still, it is thought that petroleum will disappear before 2050.

Seas and oceans cover three-quarters of the planet. Offshore oil reserves are thought to be great. They may be two or three times greater than those on land. Offshore drilling methods must then be developed. Petroleum from the North Sea took care of a third of Britain's needs in 1977. Reserves in the Gulf of Mexico, the Gulf of Thailand, and the Aegean Sea are now being studied.

In the future, petroleum will be more difficult to drill from the ground. This would be true even if the world reserves were greater.

Here is an example. In 1968, a huge deposit was found in northern Alaska. A new black gold rush began. But in that area, winter lasts for six months. In summer, mud overruns everything. Trucks get stuck in the mud. Derricks sink into it. Because of these conditions, the pipelines must be raised. Icebergs constantly threaten underwater "Christmas trees."

In ten years, the future of petroleum may be found in sand, shale, sandstone, and bituminous limestone. Petroleum will be harder to take out of these rocks. It will also be hard to refine.

GAS

When was manufactured gas first used?

Gas was first manufactured in the late eighteenth century. Scientists found that gas could be made from heating coal without air. This process is the same as that used to make coke from coal. For that reason, the gas was called coke oven gas, or coal gas.

Many people experimented with the gas. One of these people was William Murdock, a British engineer. Murdock is known as the father of the gas industry. In 1792, Murdock was already lighting his home with the gas. But in general, coal gas was first used for public lighting. One of its first demonstrations, in fact, was held at Westminster Bridge, England, in 1813. Gas-lit street lights and public buildings soon followed. In the beginning, however, gas was looked upon doubtfully. People hired to light the lamps refused. They were afraid the gas would explode.

But soon, the new means of lighting did catch on. From public places, it soon entered homes. A new method of transportation was needed. At first, the gas was stored in elastic water skins. These were stowed in huge wagons of thin metal. The wagons were pulled by several sets of horses. Each of these water skins was bound by straps. A long tube fitted with a tap controlled the gas inside. At each house, the coach-

Gas was first used for lighting needs in the early 1800s. Lamplighters (below) lit the street lamps each evening. Later, gas was carried to homes by horse and wagon.

man plugged a tube into the customer's tank. The tap was opened and the straps were tightened. This forced the gas from the skin into the tank.

Eventually, someone thought of putting the gas into cylinders. These also stacked well into the wagon. They made distributing gas much easier.

The use of gas continued to grow. Trains, steamboats, and ocean-going ships carried gas in bottles. Soon, delivering gas by horse-drawn wagon did not meet the demand. People dreamed of piping gas. It would travel directly from factory to home. This called for pipes to be placed below the sidewalks. This caused a storm of protest. People were very afraid of possible fires or explosions. (A few had actually occurred in London and Paris.) Others were annoyed by the smell and bother. Petitions were passed around to prevent the construction.

But soon, dangerous leaks were plugged. The pipes were in place. The sidewalks were patched. The protests died down. Then everyone seemed happy to "abandon themselves to gas." In houses and apartments everywhere, people had gas for every need. There was gas for lighting, cooking, and even heating.

Why did natural gas replace coal gas?

There are two basic types of gas: manufactured gas and natural gas. Manufactured gas, as you have seen, is made from other products. Coal gas is made from coal. Other types of petroleum products can also produce gases. Natural gas, as its name suggests, is natural. It comes from deposits found in the earth.

The natural gas industry began in the United States. It began to grow in the 1920s. Before that, oil, manufactured gas, and electricity had kept attention from natural gas. But large natural gas deposits found in Texas, Louisiana, and Oklahoma changed that. People began to look at natural gas again.

Employees of the gas company began to meet with the customers. "Natural gas will replace coal gas," they announced. Soon, the old heaters were replaced with new ones. When the last of the coal gas had burned, natural gas filled the pipes. It entered people's homes for the first time.

About the same time, new gas pipes were introduced. These pipes were seamless, electrically welded steel pipes. Because of this, these pipes were much stronger than the first pipes. They could carry greater amounts of gas for longer distances.

But the use of natural gas grew for other reasons. Mainly, it was cheaper than manufactured gas. It needed less treatment, or refining, for use. It was also much better for heating. Natural gas gave about twice as much heat as manufactured gas did. Therefore, people used about half as much. This also led to its importance in cooking.

For all of these reasons, natural gas began to replace other gases in many uses. This was especially true in the United States. Almost all of the gas in the United States is natural gas.

How is natural gas formed?

Scientists believe that natural gas was formed billions of years ago. Like oil, gas is also believed to have formed from plankton. These tiny plants and animals lived in the shallow waters. As they died, they sank to the ocean floor. Their remains were covered over by sediment. This layer protected the plankton remains from the air. Layers built upon layers. The weight, and other factors such as heat, bacteria, etc., may have changed the plankton to oil and gas. No one knows exactly how these products formed. Many experts accept this explanation.

While exploring for oil, oilmen often found gas trapped under the oil deposits. This is not too surprising. If both gas and oil come from plankton, they would be found together. But this is not always the case. Gas is very light. It can slip through the smallest crack and fill up another. Petroleum, however, is heavier. It does not flow as freely. But the same impenetrable, or solid, rocks trap them both.

Sometimes gas escapes to the surface by itself. In ancient times, people made use of these gas leaks. The priests of the Fire Worshippers sect in Persia used this gas. The area around a leak was covered with clay. This prevented the gas from escaping. After that, the priest built his house on this waterproof ground. Inside, the priest made narrow openings in the clay with reeds. The reeds were smeared with lime and corked with plugs. When light or heat was needed, a reed was unplugged. The priest then simply lit the escaping gas.

Does that amaze you? This is basically how today's pipes bring gas to your home. A tap takes the place of the plug. There is one main difference, however. The Fire Worshippers did not have to measure the gas they used. It was free.

Billions of years ago, small animals and plants died and sank to the ocean floor. These organisms, called plankton, were covered by many layers of sediment. Scientists believe that under these layers, plankton was changed to petroleum and gas.

How is gas transported and stored?

Drilling for natural gas is a tricky process. Transporting the gas after removing it from the earth is even more difficult. Sometimes, a company's customers live across the sea. This calls for a fleet of ships called gas tankers. But this transportation must also be profitable. A lot of gas must be stored at one time. Natural gas is often stored as a liquid. It becomes a liquid when its temperature is lowered. Liquid natural gas (LNG) takes up much less room than natural gas. A tanker holds about six hundred times more LNG than natural gas.

Transporting natural gas has several steps. First of all, the pipeline carries the gas to factories near a port. In the factories, the gas is changed into a liquid. Then it is loaded onto a gas tanker and carried across the sea. At its destination, the LNG is unloaded. Now it must be returned to its gaseous form. Simply raising its temperature will do this.

Of course, not all of this gas is used immediately. Some of it is stored. Having a reserve is very important. To understand why, think about your day. Today, like every day, you got dressed in the morning and had breakfast. At noon you had lunch. Dinner was in the early evening. Your use of gas followed your timetable. Thousands or millions of other people did the same as you did. Yet, no matter how many people needed gas at the same time, there was enough.

Pipelines alone could not meet these periods of great demand. To supply so much gas at any time, gas must be stored. Huge reserves must always be on hand. Not too long ago, you could spot these reservoirs, or tanks, of gas. They were everywhere in the city

Many tankers are built to carry petroleum. But some tankers are built to carry other sorts of liquids. This Norwegian tanker is designed to transport liquid natural gas.

and the country. These huge, metal cylinders were called gasometers. Many people considered the gasometer an eyesore. Luckily for them, gasometers have all but disappeared today.

Today, gas is often stored in underground reservoirs. Some storage areas are old natural gas deposits. Sometimes, old oil fields are used. In Colorado, an old coal mine makes an excellent storage space. With reservoirs, people's needs can easily be met. Even when there is a great demand, the reservoir does not run short.

Can natural gas reserves be exhausted?

The natural gas industry is a growing one. As recently as 1960, huge reserves were found and tapped. But the uses for natural gas are also growing.

The main natural gas producing countries are Russia, the United States, Canada, and the Netherlands. Some countries like France, Belgium, and Italy have few deposits of natural gas. These countries must import it. The gas-producing countries are exporting more and more natural gas all the time.

Like any resource, natural gas can also be used up. For this reason, people are concerned about the reserves. In the United States, gas reserves will last many years. But because more is needed every day, no one knows how long it will last. Scientists continue to look for more efficient uses of natural gas.

Gas was originally stored in large tanks called gasometers. Today, these bulky containers are rarely seen.

Gas is now stored in huge underground reservoirs, or tanks. Many storage areas are old gas or oil fields. The storage area pictured here is found at Saint-Illiers, France. Only some buildings can be seen at the surface. The United States has about 380 underground reservoirs.

WIND ENERGY

What is the wind?

It is a warm summer day. A crowd has gathered on the beach along a coastal mountain. Some 5,000 feet (1,500 m) above them, colored spots dot the sky. They are hang gliders. Hang gliding is a sport in which a rider is harnessed to a kite-like glider. Descending from a cliff or hill, the riders use the wind to keep themselves in the air. Hang gliders have no motors.

Imagine that you are one of them. With a running start, you jump from the cliff, throwing yourself into space. At first, you descend slightly. Then, finding an upward air current, your hang glider climbs again. It takes you even higher than the peak from which you jumped. Hang gliding calls for a certain amount of instinct. But to be a good hang glider, you must also learn one very important skill. You must learn how to use the wind's energy.

The wind is the air that is constantly moving over the earth's surface. Sometimes the wind blows very gently. It rustles the leaves and gently bends the plants. But at other times, the wind blows hard and fast. It violently whips the ocean waves, shakes the trees, and sends the clouds flying. Mov-

ing across the land, it carries off leaves, dirt, and all sorts of loose matter. But what causes the wind?

Wind is caused by the sun's heat. The sun's energy heats the earth's surface. But the surface is not heated evenly. Certain areas are open to the sun's rays all day long. Other areas are always in the shade. Air masses above the warm areas are also warmed. When this happens, they rise. Heavier, cooler air masses flow in to fill

the spaces left by the warm air. This constant movement is what makes wind.

As the wind moves, it meets many bodies. It transmits some of its energy to each. So dead leaves and dust lift off the ground. Kites climb up in the sky. Windmills turn and sailboats move on the water with great speed. In a huge storm, roofs fly off. Trees are broken and uprooted.

The wind is a powerful source

The windmill also makes use of the wind's energy. Here old-fashioned windmills line a bank in Holland.

of energy. People have used its energy for thousands of years. Do you ever wonder who first thought of putting a sail on a boat? Before this, a ship's power came from oarsmen. These people were often slaves, prisoners of war, or convicts. When sails came into use, the oarsmen disappeared. The wind's energy replaced human energy.

In ancient times, sailors depended heavily on the wind. They traveled only when it blew in the direction they wanted to sail. But it was not long before sailors learned to sail "against the wind." That is, they sailed in the direction from which the wind was blowing. After that, boats could go anywhere . . . and return.

In the last century, sailing ships became huge, streamlined vessels. They had three, four, and even five masts. A mast is the long pole that supports the ship's sails. The masts on these ships were very tall. Huge sails of different shapes hung from them. Each sail was shaped for the way it caught the wind. Some ships, called clippers, had as many as thirty-five sails.

These ships could move at a good speed. When steam engines were first installed on ships, sailors were doubtful about them. A number of captains had the engines removed after only one trip. They felt that the engine's weight slowed the ship more than it helped it.

Today, a variety of engines have

replaced the wind's energy. These include gas engines, oil engines, and even nuclear engines. Still, a huge number of fishing boats are still equipped with sails. Even modern European fishing boats, called trawlers, keep a "support sail" on board. This sail will fill in if the motor should fail.

Today, the wind is used in many sports. Sailing just for fun is one of them. This sport has put honor back into sailing. Windsurfing is another wind-powered sport. It is a water version of hang gliding. But here, the "wing" is a sail. It is held vertically against the mast. The windsurfer stands upright on a surfboard, working the sail. Moving it in this way, the sail catches the greatest amount of wind.

Where were windmills built?

When you were little, you probably played with toy windmills. Pinwheels, as they were called, were multi-colored plastic toys. They had four wings that revolved on the end of a stick. To make them turn, all you needed was to "catch the wind." The slightest breeze filled the four wings and made the pinwheel spin. True windmills react the same way.

Windmills are another way in which people use the wind's energy. They are known to have existed already in seventh century Iran or in Afghanistan. In those countries, the wind always blows in the same direction on the plains. These windmills were stationary. But in Europe, wind direction constantly changes. The wind changes direction according to the season or the day. Sometimes it even shifts from one hour to the next. Because of this, the Europeans could not use stationary windmills. They needed windmills that could work nonstop despite the changing winds.

The engineers of the Middle Ages came up with an idea. They put the windmill's wings, or sometimes the entire mill, on a pivot. This allowed the windmill to shift as the wind did. The windmill's use spread quickly. In the twelfth century, 120 windmills were found in the western part of Belgium. There, in the community of Ypres, the land was very flat. Because of this, the rivers ran very slowly. They could not provide as much energy as the windmills could.

The windmills soon spread to Holland. There, in the winter, the canals were also useless. But Holland's windmills did more than grind wheat or corn. They were also used as pumps to dry the polders. Polders were large areas of half-submerged land. The people used the windmills to reclaim this land from the sea.

In the valleyed countries, windmills were built on hills. There the winds were stronger than at ground level. The energy, then, was also greater.

The windpump is another way to use the wind's energy. In countries such as Morocco, the windpump supplies an otherwise dry area with water.

The windmills have disappeared little by little in Europe. But there are still some left. These can be found on certain plains where the wind blows constantly. In Holland, for example, the canals still freeze every winter. In Crete, other energy forms are still scarce.

What is the future of wind energy?

The wind is a valuable source of energy. It is free. It does not pollute. Best of all, it cannot be used up. But it is also an unpredictable source of energy. Sometimes it blows too hard. Other times, it barely blows at all.

The wind is also a very powerful energy source. Scientists have measured the strength of all winds blowing on earth at one time. This amount is six thousand times greater than the world's energy needs during that same time. This energy could be used if it could be stored. The only known method of storing it is to change it into electrical energy. This is done with a device called an aerogenerator. An aerogenerator is a modern windmill. It has a huge propeller-type wheel with two or three blades. This is mounted on top of a tall tower. The wheel is connected to an electrical generator. As the wind turns the wheel, electricity is produced.

But it would take many aerogenerators to provide a large amount of energy. The noise this would make would be deafening. It would force any people living nearby to move. So this idea would only work in totally deserted areas. But small centers working with the same idea could be used.

HYDRAULIC ENERGY

What is the water cycle?

Water, as you know, is also an important energy source. It can be used to produce both mechanical and electrical power. You may have wondered if it, too, can be used up. Luckily, water as an energy source cannot be used up. Thanks to the water cycle, it is always renewed.

The water cycle is the unending circulation of the earth's water. These waters move from the oceans, to the air, to the land, and back to the oceans. Years ago, scientists thought that the sun would someday evaporate all the water on earth. It was not until recently that the water cycle was really understood.

To understand the water cycle, try this experiment. Hold a plate upside down over a saucepan of boiling water. The steam which rises clings to the plate. Quickly, large drops appear and fall onto the stove. You have just created rain.

The sun evaporates water from the ocean. The water, in the form of vapor, rises. It later falls back to the earth. Then it is rain, snow, or some other form of moisture. Some of the moisture is absorbed by the earth's surface. It nourishes the pastures, forests, flowers, and grain. Some rain soaks further into the earth. It returns to springs and wells. Most of the rain, however, falls into the oceans. In time, the cycle will begin again.

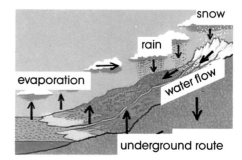

An average of 12 cu. miles (48 cu. km) of water evaporates per hour. Of this, 10 cu. miles (40 cu. km) come from the oceans. The rest comes from the continents.

Why were waterwheels built on rivers?

Waterwheels have been used since ancient times. They were one of the first devices used to capture water's energy. Most waterwheels were huge wheels that hung on a frame over a river. There the waterwheel had the swift speed of the river to power it. The waterwheel used the falling water's energy. This energy was changed into mechanical energy. As the water fell on the wheel's blades, the wheel turned.

Early waterwheels were used for grinding wheat and other grains. They were also used in making oil from olives or nuts. As years passed, the waterwheel was improved. In the Middle Ages, the wheel was used for powering other machinery. Unfortunately, waterwheels were not always dependable energy sources. The amount of power the wheel provided sometimes depended on the amount of water available. Droughts or floods caused many problems.

Many people think that waterwheels were only found along rivers in the quiet countryside. But they were also found in the city. There they were tied to a bank, sometimes in a horizontal position. Sometimes one of them would break loose. A runaway waterwheel could cause a lot of damage. Waterwheels were also found under the arches of bridges. There the current was usually strong. The wheels turned swiftly and picked up speed. In 1323, thirteen such wheels were counted in Paris.

Today, it is hard to imagine what life was like around these wheels. Sometimes, industrial centers sprang up around them. There were workshops where skins were tanned. In others, tools were ground and metals were polished. These centers became places to meet, to get supplies, and to do business.

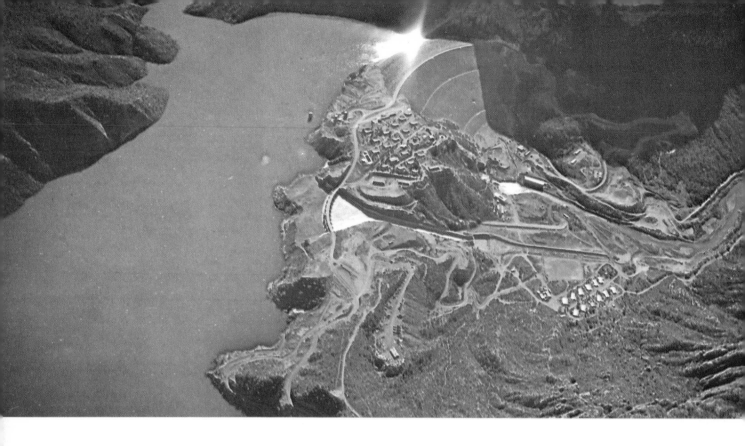

The Cabra Corral Dam is found in Argentina. When a dam is placed across a river or stream, the stored water creates a lake.

What is hydroelectric power?

As you know, moving water can be an excellent energy source. That is why waterwheels are built along rivers and streams. Hydroelectric power is also provided by water. Water stored behind dams runs huge hydroelectric plants. Simply put, hydroelectric power is electricity generated by falling water.

The energy that a water reservoir has depends on its depth. The deeper the water behind the dam, the more energy it has. This explains the height of some large dams. Some of them are as much as 328 feet (100 m) high. Most often, the center of electricity is found below the dam. Sometimes it is part of the structure.

Dams can help a nation make industrial progress. The power from a dam can bring a nation needed energy. But building a dam can also cause problems. It can greatly change the surrounding area. It can also affect its plant and animal life. The Malpasset Dam in France broke on December 2, 1959. It gave way under the water's weight. Four hundred people were killed when their village flooded. The valley around the dam was in ruin for years.

To date, the Aswan Dam is the world's largest. It is built in upper Egypt on the Nile River. Its construction brought many changes. More than fifty thousand people had to move. Ancient temples also had to be moved stone by stone. Moving these was very ex-pensive and time-consuming. But this was not the most serious of changes. The river itself was changed. The Nile River is known for its floods. Each year it flows over its banks and deposits lime on the land. When the water retreats, the lime leaves the land fertile. This flooding has gone on for thousands of years. Since the dam was built, the floods have almost disappeared. This change has hurt millions of small farmers. They depended on the river's floods to nourish their land.

In industrial nations, energy needs keep on growing. All the hydroelectric power is not enough to meet these needs.

GEOTHERMAL ENERGY

Are there natural hot water reserves under the ground?

The earth's temperature increases with depth. Miners know this from their work. The further down they go into mine shafts, the hotter it gets. The temperature rises 37°F (3°C) for every 328 feet (100 m). Sometimes it rises as much as 41° or 50°F (5° or 10°C).

Water flowing into underground rivers and streams is also affected by temperature changes. The deeper it goes into the earth, the hotter it will also be. Sometimes this water will come across an impermeable, or solid, layer. Clay is an example of this. The water will stop there. It will form a pool between that layer and those above it. Water reservoirs are formed this way. At 5,000 feet (1,500 m) down, the water may be as hot as 176°F (80°C).

These reservoirs are called low energy deposits. They are a source of geothermal power. Geothermal power is created when water comes in contact with the earth's internal heat. The water, which turns to steam, can be used for heating. It can also be used in making electricity. Water used in geothermal power comes from deep within the earth. Bringing it to the surface can be difficult. Luckily, the water sometimes rises by itself.

The oldest known of these wells is found in Europe. It dates back to 1126. The first one was discovered while digging in the convent

Geothermal power plants take energy from underground hot water reservoirs. These non-polluting plants can even generate electricity.

of Chartreux in Artois. This region is found in northern France. The area has lent its name to these hot water reservoirs. They are now known as "Artesian wells." People soon found that the land in Artois was rich in water. Water could be found only 23 feet (7 m) below the surface. In some villages, each house had its own well.

More recent uses for naturally heated water can be found. In the last century, a German inventor made use of one of these hot springs. Channeling the water through pipes, the inventor devised his own heating system. He was able to heat his whole workshop. When the temperature outside hit zero, the workshop stayed comfortably warm. This has worked in other cases, too. Greenhouses, hospitals, workshops, prisons, and homes have all been successfully heated this way.

Geothermal energy is another source of non-polluting energy. In some cases, it is also a cheaper source of energy.

How does the earth's heat generate electricity?

Not all hot springs are underground streams or lakes. Some hot springs take the form of a geyser. A geyser is a spring that spouts hot water and steam to the earth's surface. Some geysers spout at regular times. Others are very random. Here, the Norris Geyser in Wyoming (United States) begins to spout.

Very hot, liquid rocks are found in pockets in the earth. These pockets, called magmatic pockets, often occur in areas where volcanoes are active. They may also form along fault lines, where tremors are common.

Water flows and collects at different levels above these pockets. This water may grow as hot as 572°F (300°C). Water normally boils at 212°F (100°C). If you heat water in a pan, it will boil at this temperature. But this is true when the water is under normal pressure. The atmosphere in which you live is considered normal pressure. When that pressure increases, however, water boils at a higher temperature.

Underground water is some- times trapped between molten pockets and impermeable rock layers. In these pockets, both heat and pressure increase. As they increase, the water tries to escape. It follows the faults and cracks along the earth's crust. Where it can, it bursts forth at the surface. This is how geysers form.

This type of water reservoir is called a high energy field. It can be used to produce electricity. But to do this, the energy must be converted. People tap this energy by drilling into these water reservoirs. The steam is then directed into a steam turbine. There it is changed into electricity. Many countries have worked with this idea.

What is the future of geothermal energy?

In the future, scientists may find more uses for geothermal energy. But it is not ever expected to supply even two percent of the world's energy needs. In fact, it is mostly used in areas rich in hot springs. But no energy source is unimportant. For this reason, all sources are explored. Since 1960, the United States has put the strength of its geysers to work. In Reykjavik, the capital of Iceland, the entire town is heated by water from geysers.

The difference between high- and low-energy deposits is the temperature. These burning waters and steamy springs have very different qualities. Some springs have very pure water. Water from these can be used to fill swimming pools. Later, it can be dumped into the sewer. But other springs contain damaging salt water. This water cannot be run through pipes.

In some areas, there is no underground steam. This happens when water is not present. In these cases, geothermal energy is still possible. Here, though, water is injected into the earth to absorb the heat. These steps are taken because geothermal power is a good source of energy. The power plants do not burn anything. So there are no pollutants put into the air.

ELECTRICITY

How does an electric battery work?

A dispute between two Italian scientists led to the invention of the battery. One scientist, Luigi Galvani, was an anatomy professor at the University of Bologna, Italy. Anatomy is a science that deals with the structure of organisms. In 1786, Galvani began working with electricity. Sometime before, he had noticed a strange reaction in dissected frogs. He had hung the legs of a dead frog on a copper hook. This he hung over an iron railing. When the frog's legs touched the railing, they twitched. Galvani felt this was caused by electricity in the animal.

Another scientist, Alessandro Volta, did not accept Galvani's idea. He believed that the metals themselves caused the frog's legs to twitch. Copper and iron, he pointed out, are two very different metals. Under certain conditions, he felt, they would produce current. Volta tried many different combinations of metals to prove this. In 1800, he stacked up a series of discs. Copper and zinc discs, and acid-soaked cloth were piled one on top of another. When he touched the top of this stack, he felt movement. This movement became stronger if more discs were used. With this, Volta created the first real battery. Today, it is known as the Volta battery.

Volta's electric energy was actually caused by a chemical reac-

Getting light from electricity was the subject of many experiments in the 1800s. This 1844 etching shows the beginning of electric lighting.

tion. The scientist did not know it at the time. This fact was discovered later. To make a battery, two different metals are placed into a liquid. The liquid is a conductor of current. This simple operation causes a reaction. The reaction gives off chemical energy. This is immediately transformed into electric energy. A battery, then, is a generator of current.

But these reactions have some other results, too. They cause deposits to build up around the conductors. This causes the battery to lose power. Today's batteries are better than Volta's were. But even these do not last forever.

1800: Volta's battery was a column of copper and zinc discs. They were separated by acid-soaked stoppers.

New York at night.

How was electric lighting invented?

In 1802, Sir Humphrey Davy, an Englishman, came up with an idea for lighting. Davy's idea called for passing an electric spark between two conductors stuck in a battery. To this he added a small charcoal rod at the end of each conductor. All of this was enclosed in a glass globe.

By the end of 1844, people were gathering in crowds to see this lighting. Inventors spent their time imagining how to light an entire city. Some of them came up with successful ideas. But other ideas were not practical. One scientist suggested setting up one huge light on a column to light a city. Another suggested projecting the light's beam on the clouds. The reflected light would light a city. But this overlooked the fact that the sky is not always cloudy.

Some inventors dreamed of making the light useful to everyone. They hoped to one day have electric lighting in every home. But for this to be possible, there were problems to be solved. For one thing, the light at the center of the bulb was very powerful. For the home, this overpowering light would have to be reduced. Secondly, the electricity had to be considered. Getting it to the customers remained a problem.

The American inventor, Thomas A. Edison, solved both problems. After much work, Edison refined the light bulb. A very fine carbon wire controlled the bulb's glow. His work was the model for

This room is equipped with Edison electric light. Do not try to light it with a match. Simply turn the switch on the wall near the door.

This card was displayed in an American hotel at the turn of the century.

Edison bulbs.

the modern day bulb. Edison also developed one of the first electrical power plants. The plant, which opened in 1882, generated and distributed electricity. It made electricity possible and affordable. For his work, Edison is often thought of as the inventor of the electric lamp.

At first, electric lighting had been used only for entertainment. It was used to light statues, parties, theater events, and similar gatherings. Improvements on the light, however, made it much more useful. For one thing, with the light, work could be done at night. Before this, people had to rely on candles, fires, gas lights, or oil lamps for light at night. Electric lighting was also an improvement in mine work. This lighting reduced the danger of explosions. Even sailors made use of electric lighting. Between 1860 and 1865, electric lights replaced oil lamps on many ships.

Electricity is used in many forms of transportation. Some streetcars, subways, and railroads are electrically powered. Some of these railway systems can move as fast as 155 miles (250 km) an hour.

An aerotrain is one possibility for future train travel. It rides on a cushion of air above a single rail. The aerotrain is very fast. A model aerotrain operates near Orleans, France. It moves as fast as 170 miles (274 km) an hour. Unfortunately, it uses a great amount of energy.

How was the electric motor discovered?

Volta's electric battery has been experimented with since its invention. Many researchers have tried to change its electrical energy into mechanical energy. Some interesting results came out of these experiments. One inventor built a battery-powered boat. It worked, but it could go no faster than 3 miles (5 km) an hour. Worse yet, fumes from the battery nearly killed everyone on board.

Still, people dreamed of building the ideal engine. A Belgian electrician named Zenobe Gramme found the solution. Gramme and his associate, Hippolyte Fontaine, invented a special steam machine. This machine could run two generators. A generator is a device that changes mechanical energy into electrical energy. The men thought that if one quit working, the other could replace it. But while one generator was producing electricity, the other was also in motion. It was not making electricity, but it was working. Gramme and Fontaine realized that their gadget was reversible. It could change its own electrical energy into mechanical energy. The first electric motor had been born.

One of the first uses of this engine was in 1879. Visitors to the Berlin Exposition got a first look at a small electric train. The train was hooked to an electrical wire hanging above it. It was able to carry passengers and move at 7 miles (12 km) an hour. Germany soon replaced its horse-drawn carriages with trains. In London, a steam train already ran underground. An electric model was installed in 1887. These electric trains were brought to the United States in 1895.

A turbine engine in an electrical plant.

Can electric energy be stored?

Imagine the electricity going out in a big city on a winter evening. Houses would be without heat or light. The television and the radio would not work. The streets would be a mess without traffic lights to control the traffic. Thousands of factories would have to shut down without power for their machines. In high-rise buildings, elevators would stop. The railroad stations and airports would be without signal lights. Trains would stop in open country. Airplanes would be grounded.

Does this sound impossible? It isn't. A breakdown like this has actually happened. It took place in New York (United States) on November 9, 1965. More recently, the city had a "blackout" on July 13, 1977.

These days, people are dependent on electricity. This is especially true of those in cities. But few people use electricity where it is made. Electricity must be used at the moment it is generated. It cannot be stored. Most often, electricity is made far from where it is distributed.

An example of this can be found in Sweden. Important hydroelectric plants are found in the northern part of the country. There the land is well-suited for making hydroelectric energy. But this is not the case everywhere. In Sweden, some big cities are more than 500 miles (800 km) south of these plants. Electricity must be brought to them. Some of these are rich in coal. Materials like lignite and peat could be used to generate electricity. In these cases, it is easier to build a thermal plant near the cities. Solid or liquid materials (such as coal or petroleum) are then brought in to fuel them.

Another option for meeting a city's electrical needs is to use two kinds of plants together. Sometimes, a thermal plant and a hydro-electrical plant work together.

How is electricity transmitted?

Once electricity is generated, it must then be transmitted, or carried, to its users. Huge amounts of electrical energy are produced in power stations. This energy must then be sent out over a wide area.

In the 1800s, people began working with the idea of sending electricity out over wires. One French engineer, Marcel Deprez, thought of using telegraph wires for this purpose. The wires carried the electricity for about 12 miles (20 km). At the other end, Deprez found that the electricity had lost much power. This power loss was caused by the line's resistance to the electricity flowing through it.

To be sent long distances, electricity must be "pushed." Very high voltage, or power, is needed to do this. But when the electricity reaches the homes of local users, lower voltages are needed. An electrical current's voltage is lowered or highered by a device known as a transformer. Electricity moves from the plant to substations along high-voltage wires. In the stations and along the lines, transformers continually lower the voltage. By the time it reaches a home, it may have gone from hundreds of thousands of volts to 240 volts.

Electricity comes into the house through a meter. The current also passes through a fuse box. This controls the flow of electricity to home appliances.

Electricity must be carried over long distances. A network of high voltage wires carries it from the plant to substations. There the voltage will be reduced for use in homes, factories, etc.

Electric cars are a non-polluting form of transportation. They are also cheap to run.

Will electricity someday power cars?

You are in a train station, waiting for the train. A vehicle loaded with baggage comes toward you along the platform. It is driven by just one man. You can barely hear the vehicle's motor. It stops and then moves off quietly. As it passes, you do not smell burning gas or oil.

This is an electric motor. It gets its energy from batteries. Electric cars have several advantages over gasoline cars. For one thing, electric cars cost less to run. They also do not use gas. So running them does not affect oil reserves. But most of all, electric cars cause no pollution. So why not make all cars this way?

Well, electric cars also have some problems. One thing is their speed. An electric car's fastest speed is no more than 50 miles (80 km) an hour. They also have huge batteries, so there is not much passenger space. Finally,

electric cars must be recharged often. They can travel about 60 miles (97 km) between charges.

Still, experiments on electric vehicles continue. Certain buses run on electrical energy now. For part of a journey, the bus is powered by wires running above it. This is the way some subways and trams work. This recharges the battery on the bus while it moves. Then, when the bus leaves the lines, it is powered by its own battery.

These buses carry about twenty-four people. They can move as fast as 37 miles (60 km) per hour. But they usually travel about half this fast. Still, the future for electrical vehicles is bright. Scientists continue to work with them because of their advantages. Someday, a smaller, more powerful battery may be developed. Then the electric vehicle may find widespread use.

NUCLEAR ENERGY

What is an atom?

All living things are made of matter. Atoms are the "building blocks" of all matter. Solids, liquids, and gases can be broken down into tiny particles. The atom's name comes from the Greek word *atomos,* meaning "uncuttable." It was named by the Greek scholar Democritus. Democritus believed that all matter could be reduced to these tiny particles. But the atom itself, he believed, could not be broken down any further. It was uncuttable.

Atoms are very small. They cannot be seen with the naked eye, or with even a simple microscope. The atom, however, is not the solid ball that Democritus thought it was. An atom is made up of several smaller parts. These are called protons, neutrons, and electrons. Protons and neutrons are found at the atom's center. They form the nucleus. Protons are particles with a positive electrical charge. Neutrons are particles with no charge of any kind.

The nucleus is circled by particles called electrons. These are negatively charged. In an atom, the number of protons inside the nucleus matches the number of electrons outside it. This makes the atom neutral.

Atoms combine to create substances. A substance made of only one kind of atom is called an element. There are ninety elements that occur naturally in the world. Scientists have made at least fourteen elements in laboratory experiments. These elements are classified, or grouped, according to their weight, or mass. They range from hydrogen, which is the lightest, to uranium, which is the heaviest. In between are elements such as calcium, sulfur, iron, aluminum, oxygen, and so on. You probably know many of them.

But atoms of different kinds can also be combined. Two or more atoms joined together is called a molecule. An example of this is a water molecule. Each water molecule is made of two hydrogen atoms and one oxygen atom. The water molecule can be broken down into hydrogen and oxygen, but this is difficult to do. When you boil water, for example, the two do not separate.

Water and other substances made of different kinds of atoms are called chemical compounds. This sets them apart from elements which are made of only one kind of atom.

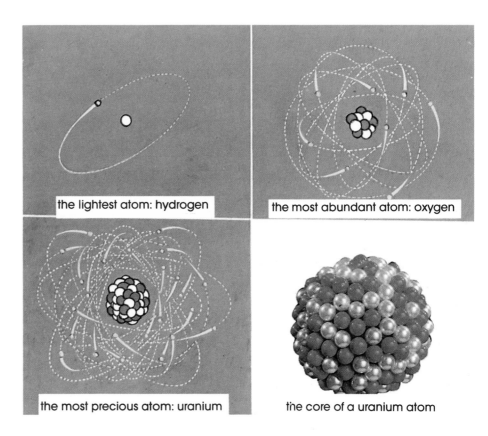

the lightest atom: hydrogen

the most abundant atom: oxygen

the most precious atom: uranium

the core of a uranium atom

What is a nuclear reaction?

The nucleus of an atom is fairly stable. It is held together by powerful forces. But sometimes, the structure of an atom does change. This change is known as a nuclear reaction. In a nuclear reaction, the nucleus gains or loses some of its protons or neutrons. It may then change into the nucleus of another element.

There are three important types of nuclear reactions. These are: radioactive decay, nuclear fission, and nuclear fusion. Radioactive decay is a natural process in which an atom's nucleus changes. The change releases energy in the form of particles and rays. Together, these are called nuclear radiation.

Nuclear reactors produce energy through nuclear fission. Fission is a process which splits the nucleus of an atom. This is done by bombarding atoms with neutrons. The neutrons cause the nucleus to split apart. This splitting, or fission, releases the energy. Most of the energy freed through fission takes the form of heat. In nuclear reactors, this heat is collected and changed into electricity.

The process of nuclear fusion, however, uses light elements. The nuclei of two lighter elements combine, or fuse, to form a third, heavier one. Together, the elements weigh less than their original combined weights. This lost weight was transformed into energy. The sun's energy is released by fusion. There, as here, temperature and pressure cause the fusion. The same thing happens in many stars.

What is nuclear energy?

Nuclear energy is the most powerful form of energy known today. It is sometimes called atomic power. This name comes from the way in which it is produced. It is the result of changes within the nucleus of an atom.

Scientists first worked with nuclear energy in the early 1900s. It was successfully released in 1942 by scientists at the University of Chicago. It has many uses today, especially in generating electricity. But people do not yet know how to use nuclear energy to its full extent. If better uses could be developed, nuclear energy could supply the world with electricity for years to come.

Nuclear energy is released mainly in the form of heat. The heat is used to make steam. In turn, the steam powers huge electrical generators. All of this is done in a device called a nuclear reactor. Nuclear reactors are found in huge nuclear power plants.

Nuclear power plants are usually found at rivers' edges or along seacoasts. There they can get the huge amounts of water needed for cooling. A plant includes several main buildings. One of these holds the reactor itself. Nuclear reactors are like huge furnaces. This "furnace," however, is fueled by uranium. With this element,

FISSION

neutron

neutron

core of an uranium atom

products of fission and energy

neutron

FUSION

core of deuterium atom

core of tritium atom

neutron

helium core and energy

1 - reactor vessel
2 - core
3 - control rods

4 - heat exchanger
5 - turbine
6 - generator

7 - condenser
8 - transformer and electrical lines

Cutaway view of a pressurized water reactor (PWR).

the reactor produces energy by fission.

Nuclear reactors in the United States have five basic parts. These include: the core, a moderator, the control rods, the coolants, and the reactor vessel. The core is the heart of the nuclear plant. It contains the nuclear fuel, which is usually a form of uranium. The actual fission occurs here.

A moderator is a material used to increase the chances of fission. This substance slows down neutrons which pass through it. Neutrons, remember, are needed to split the atoms. Slowing them down allows this to happen.

The control rods are long metal rods that actually control fission within the core. Rods are made of neutron-absorbing materials. To

slow the number of fissions down, the rods are driven deep into the core. There they absorb many neutrons. This leaves few neutrons to split any atoms. Drawing the rods out has the opposite effect.

Coolant substances absorb the heat created by fission. Coolants take the heat out of the reactor to other parts of the plant. There the heat is used to generate electricity.

The last important part of the reactor is known as the reactor vessel. This is a large steel tank that holds all the other reactor parts. It also holds the water from which steam will be made.

Many reactors in the United States are light water reactors. These reactors use plain water as both a coolant and a moderator.

One type of light water reactor is the pressurized water reactor. This reactor makes steam outside the vessel. The process begins when water is heated under pressure in the core. Pipes then take this hot water to heat exchangers outside the vessel. Heat exchangers are devices that take the heat from the pressurized water. The heat is transferred to water in a steam generator. There it is boiled and makes steam. The steam then spins the turbine paddles which drive the plant's generators. This produces an electrical current. After this, the steam is piped to a condenser. Condensers change the steam back into water. A reactor can use the same water over and over.

What is nuclear waste?

In the distance stands La Hague factory. This plant has treated nuclear wastes from French nuclear plants since 1967.

Unlike petroleum or carbon, the fuel used in a nuclear plant does not burn off completely. After fission, some of the nuclear fuel products are still highly radioactive. Radioactive substances release their energy because of changes in the nucleus of the atom. The energy is given off as invisible rays. These rays, known as radiation, can hurt living cells and tissues. This, then, is a serious drawback to using nuclear power.

Nuclear power plant wastes come from several sources. Materials from the reactor core are one source. Liquids and gases used there are another. All of these things can be very dangerous. This radioactivity can last for hundreds, even thousands, of years.

To reduce any danger to people, the wastes are moved far away. They are kept in huge, armored containers. Some of these containers are first kept in pools to cool. Others are immediately buried. But no permanent method has been chosen. For this reason, many people are against nuclear power.

Because of dangerous waste products, many people are against the use of nuclear power. Here, a crowd has gathered to demonstrate against the nuclear plants.

CONCLUSION

How can energy be conserved?

It is important to remember that energy cannot be created. It can only be changed from one form to another. As you have seen, it is possible to use up some of these energy forms. Therefore, people must learn not to waste energy of any kind. Learning to use energy wisely and not waste it is known as conservation. Conserving energy is one way to make the earth's supplies last longer.

There are many simple things that people can do to conserve energy. Keeping the thermostat set lower in the winter and higher in the summer is one. Making a heater (or air-conditioner) run non-stop is wasteful. Lowering the thermostat by even one degree in the winter saves energy.

Better insulation in buildings also saves energy. A large amount of energy escapes through ceilings, wood floors, and windows. Proper insulation saves up to half the fuel used in heating and air conditioning. Car pooling or using public transportation is another means of conservation. Even people who must drive can save energy by driving smaller cars.

Still other examples are even simpler. Do not run water needlessly from a hot or cold water tap. Turn out the lights in an empty room. Do not heat a big saucepan of water to boil just one egg. Even small things like this will help avoid wasting energy.

The cost of gasoline quadrupled in the early 1970s. Still, people have not learned enough about conserving energy.

A sorry image of Paris.

Why are cities polluted?

The word pollution refers to all the ways in which people dirty the world. Pollution comes from many sources. Bad-smelling gases that escape from cars and trucks pollute the air. Factory chimneys and heating towers belch out black clouds of smoke and dust. Chemicals and garbage dirty the water. Fertilizers and bug sprays pollute the soil. Many forms of pollution contain harmful products. These include: dust, carbon monoxide, lead, and sulfur. These are just a few examples of the way people pollute the world.

Everyone wants to stop pollution. But the problem is a difficult one. Pollution often comes from things that help people. Cars, for example, are a major source of pollution. They are noisy, smelly, and they damage the air. But cars are an important form of transportation. To help stop pollution, people could stop using cars. But most people would not want this either.

Yet pollution can be reduced in many ways. Scientists and en-gineers are trying to find less polluting ways to use energy. Governments are trying to put controls on polluting activities. Laws now force large industries to install anti-pollution systems. Factories' waste products must be disposed of properly. People's vehicles must be tested.

In the 1960s, pollution became a major concern. People are now aware of pollution and its dangers. Awareness is a first step to solving the problem.

What will the world's energy needs be in the year 2000?

Since World War II, the world's energy use has nearly doubled every fourteen years. The use of electricity rises more quickly than the others. It doubles every ten years. World use in the year 2000 could be four times what it is today. In 2100 it may be twenty-four times higher. Where will people find energy to meet these needs?

These figures account for different lifestyles. Different countries have different energy needs. Certainly, Indonesia uses less energy than America does. But imagine that everyone in the world is on the same "energy level." World energy use by 2000 would be eleven times greater than that of 1975.

Most energy disappears into the atmosphere as heat. As people's energy use increases, so does this lost heat. It is thought that this heat may one day increase the atmosphere's temperature. The amount would be slight at first. But this increase could build to a difference of several degrees. This could have dangerous effects on the world's climate. Fortunately, people all over the world now know of these dangers.

Will there be new energy sources in the future?

To meet future energy needs, new energy sources must be found. Ideally, this new energy will be non-polluting and easy to transport. It will also be easy to store for periods of high demand.

In fact, this source already exists. It is hydrogen, and it is plentiful on the earth. Hydrogen is one of two elements that make up pure water. It is possible to separate this element from the other (oxygen) for energy use.

To break down water this way, scientists will need a converter. This converter will take the chemical energy of the water and generate electrical energy. This is the reverse of what many converters now do.

But making these converters seems to be a problem. Hydrogen weakens most metals it touches. What is more, it can explode on contact with a flame. Still, experts think it will one day be used as a fuel for cars, airplanes, and small electric plants. Put into existing plants, it could meet all gas needs.

It is possible that hydrogen is the fuel of the future. People may prefer it to nuclear sources. But despite vast sources of hydrogen, this is not a good idea. It is not wise to rely on a single energy source. Using several sources avoids straining one. In fact, it would be best to have several energy sources in use at one time. Each source could be used to fill needs best suited to it. Such a plan could meet all human energy needs while preserving the earth. This idea, in fact, should be the only guide to the "energy choice" of each nation.

Estimate of the annual energy uses of the United States.

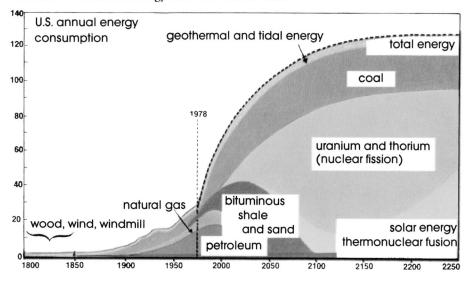

Glossary

absorber the dark, plate-like surface of a solar collector used to take in, or absorb, the sun's heat.

anthracite a hard, natural coal that is rich in carbon. Coal in its anthracite stage is very old. It burns slowly, giving off great heat, and leaves no ashes.

Archimedes a Greek mathematician and inventor.

Artesian well a well drilled deep enough into the earth to reach water that rises to the surface by internal pressure.

atom the smallest particle of matter that has distinct chemical characteristics.

bituminous coal the most common type of coal, often called soft, black coal. Bituminous coal, which is also rich in carbon, burns well but is very sooty.

coolant substances substances used in a nuclear reactor to absorb the heat created by fission. Water is often used as a coolant.

control rods long metal rods that control the fission process within the reactor core. The position of the rods determines the speed at which the fissions occur.

core the "heart" of a nuclear power plant containing the uranium (or other nuclear fuel). Fission takes place within the core.

core sample a sample of drilling mud taken with a drill which shows the presence of oil.

current a flow of electric charge.

derrick a framework erected over a drilled hole which is used to support the drilling equipment. Derricks are often used in drilling for oil.

electron a small, negatively charged particle circling the nucleus of an atom.

energy converter a device used to change energy from one form into another. Converters can be very simple devices such as a bicycle pedal or a waterwheel blade. They can also be complex devices such as steam or electrical engines.

fission a type of nuclear reaction in which the nucleus (core) of an atom is split into two nearly equal parts. Fission is the only type of nuclear reaction scientists have learned to control. With it, they can produce tremendous energy.

fusion a type of nuclear reaction that uses the atoms of light elements. In fusion, the nuclei of two lighter atoms combine, or fuse, to form a third, heavier nucleus. The sun's energy is released through fusion.

generator a machine used to change mechanical energy into electrical energy.

geyser a natural hot spring that ejects steam and hot water.

greenhouse effect the process by which the atmosphere helps trap the sun's heat. Like the glass of a greenhouse, the earth's atmosphere allows sunlight through to the earth's surface. The light warms the earth, but the heat it creates cannot easily pass through the atmosphere and escape into space. The earth is warmed by this trapped heat.

impermeable not permitting passage, such as of a fluid, through a substance.

impurities materials of an inferior or worthless quality that are mixed with more valuable materials. In iron ore, for example, valuable materials such as iron and steel may be mixed with impurities like sand and rocks.

light water reactor a nuclear reactor which uses water as both its coolant substance and its moderator. Many reactors in the United States are this type.

lignite a brownish black coal between the peat and bituminous coal stages. Lignite is loose-grained and does not heat as well as later coal forms.

moderator a material used to increase the chances of fission. A moderator slows down the neutrons which pass through it, allowing them to split atoms.

molecule the simplest structural unit formed when two or more different atoms join together.

neutron one of two kinds of particles found in the nucleus of an atom. The neutron is an electrically neutral particle.

nuclear reaction a process by which the structure of an atom's nucleus is changed. Fission, fusion, and radioactive decay are three major forms of nuclear reaction.

nuclear reactor a device in which nuclear reactions can be created and controlled for the purpose of creating nuclear energy.

nucleus the core of an atom, usually consisting of particles known as protons and neutrons.

nutrient something that nourishes.

ore a mineral or rock from which a valuable substance, such as metal, comes.

peat partially carbonized vegetable matter. Peat is considered to be the first stage in the formation of coal.

peat bog a huge deposit of peat.

photosynthesis the process by which plants combine energy from sunlight with carbon dioxide and water to make food. In the process, the plants release oxygen as a by-product.

plankton floating masses of tiny plant and animal life found in a water body.

porous full of many small holes or openings through which liquid can pass.

prospecting exploring an area, especially for mineral deposits.

proton one of two types of particles found in the nucleus of an atom. Protons have a positive charge.

radioactive decay a natural nuclear reaction by which an atom's nucleus changes into the nucleus of another. The change releases energy in the form of particles and rays (nuclear radiation).

refinery an industrial plant where crude substances, especially petroleum, are purified.

rickets a disease of children resulting from a lack of vitamin D and characterized by soft, deformed bones.

slag heaps hills of leftover materials from mining operations.

smalls fine, dust-like particles of coal resulting from cutting, cleaning, and transporting coal processes.

smelt to melt or fuse ores in order to extract the metals contained in them.

solar cell device for converting sunlight into electricity.

solar energy energy given off by the sun. This energy is produced by nuclear reactions that occur at the sun's core.

solar flare a burst of light on the sun's surface. Flares release huge amounts of energy.

strip mining an open form of mining in which the coal seams run close to ground level and are exposed by the stripping of the topsoil.

water cycle the never-ending movement of the earth's water from the oceans, to the air, to the land, and back to the oceans again.

INDEX